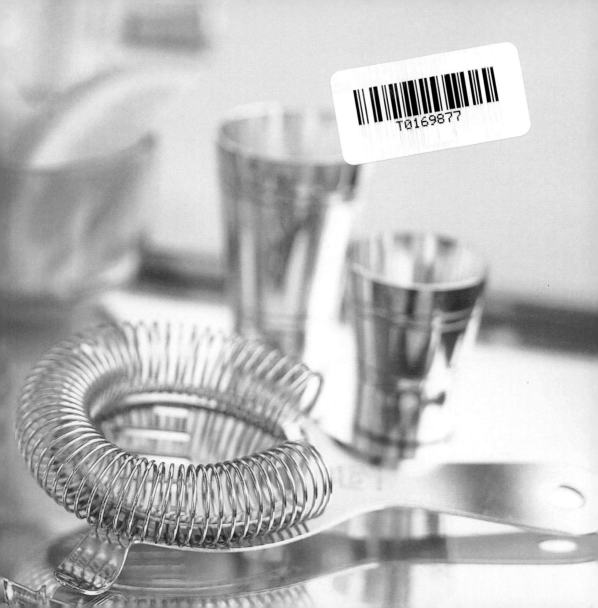

T0169877

BRANDY
cocktails

STUART WALTON

LORENZ BOOKS

Contents

Introduction

Brandy is the spirit that results from the distillation of fermented grapes. Put that way, it sounds rather basic, but its finest products are among the most revered productions of the spirit world. At the very top are the speciality cognacs and armagnacs of western and southwestern France, given many years cask-ageing until they are mellowed to wondrous softness of texture and depth of flavour, just right for sipping meditatively at the close of a memorable evening.

Cognac has long been associated with a certain swaggering demeanour, and its reputation as the drink of heroes, according to the eighteenth-century writer Dr Samuel Johnson, is sealed by the classification of one of its higher grades as Napoleon brandy. Armagnac has always had a much less aristocratic self-image, although its best grades, vintage-dated or labelled Hors d'Age, are just as opulent. Versions of brandy are also produced, though, pretty much anywhere that has a wine industry, including Spain, Germany, Mexico and the United States. Greece has its Metaxa, a brandy blended with undistilled wine, which comes in star-rated quality grades up to seven, and South America's speciality is pisco, a Peruvian and Chilean grape spirit that dates back to the days of the Spanish conquests.

Brandy is one of those commodities that can't be produced cheaply and well. Basic grades, simply labelled 'French brandy' rather than cognac or armagnac, are frankly horrible. Understandably, you won't want to use the most refined and costly products in a cocktail mix, but don't dip below the everyday grade of cognac known as VS (Very Special), which has had a minimum two years' barrel-ageing.

Incidentally, if you are enjoying an after-dinner tot of fine brandy as it comes, without ice or any other adulterant, try serving it in a narrow-sided small glass, like a sherry copita. It's incomparably kinder to the drink than pouring it into one of the traditional old balloon glasses, which because of the greater surface area of the liquid, force it to assault the senses with a nostril-prickling blast of nothing more than raw 40% spirit.

Right: The traditional way to drink cognac is unadulterated with mixers or ice.

What is brandy?

Strictly speaking, the term brandy applies to any grape-based spirit distilled from wine. The most famous of all true brandies is cognac, named after a town in the Charente region of western France. It was to here that traders from northern Europe came in the 17th century, putting in at the port of La Rochelle to take delivery of consignments of salt. They inevitably took some of the region's thin, acidic wine with them as well. Because of tax regulations, and to save space in the ships, the wines were boiled to reduce their volume and then reconstituted with water on arrival. It came to be noticed that the Charente wines positively benefited from the reduction process, and it was a short step from this to actual distillation.

Such was the fame and the premium paid for the distilled wines of the Charente that they came to have many imitators. None, however, could match the precise local conditions in which cognac is made. The chalky soils, maritime climate and ageing in barrels of Limousin oak were what gave it the pre-eminence it still enjoys.

France's other brandy of note, armagnac, is made in the south-west. Although not as widely known as cognac, it has its own special cachet, and is preferred by many as the better digestif.

There are grape brandies produced all over Europe and the Americas, the best of which are generally made by pot-still distillation.

Cognac

The Cognac region covers two *départements* in western France: inland Charente, and coastal Charente-Maritime. Cognac is a small town close to the border between the two. The vineyards are sub-divided into six areas, the best being Grande Champagne and Petite Champagne.

First among Cognac's entrepreneurs was Jean Martell, a Jersey-born opportunist who, in 1715, turned away from a life of crime (smuggling) in order to found the house that still bears his name. Other leading brands are Hennessy, Courvoisier, Hine, Otard and Rémy Martin.

Above left: The basic Rémy Martin is a VSOP grade of cognac. Above right: Martell, the oldest house in Cognac, is a brand leader.

The relative qualities of cognacs depend on the length of time they have been aged. No *appellation contrôlée* cognac may be blended from spirits less than two years old. At the bottom rung of the classification is VS (designated by three stars on the label), which may contain brandies as young as three years old. ▶

The next stage up is VSOP, Very Special (or Superior) Old Pale, a 19th-century British term. This is five-star cognac because the youngest spirit it contains has spent at least five years in wood.

Those cognacs blended from minimum six-year-old spirits may be entitled XO, or given one of the producers' own designations: Réserve, Extra, Cordon Bleu,

Below left: The term "Hors d'Age" on an armagnac label denotes very long cask-ageing.
Below right: Lepanto is Spain's leading brandy, made by Gonzales Byass of sherry fame.

Above: Barrels of cognac stacked to the ceilings at the Otard distillery, Chateâu des Valois, Cognac.

Paradis or, classically, Napoleon – named because the bottles once contained brandies aged since Bonaparte's day.

Armagnac

Once seen merely as France's "other brandy", armagnac is made in Gascony in the south-west. Of the three sub-regions – Bas-Armagnac, Ténarèze and Haut-Armagnac – the first is considered the best. Armagnac is a more venerable product than cognac, distillation in the region having been reliably dated back to the 1400s. While cognac is made largely from the Ugni Blanc grape, armagnac's base wine is made from a blend of several varieties. A local black oak (as distinct from Limousin) is used for the maturation, and the continuous still is widely used to distil the spirit.

So inextricably linked with armagnac was the continuous still that, for a long time, it was the only authorized apparatus. It yields a spirit rich in the aromatic impurities that promote character, which is why armagnac is noticeably more fragrant – biscuity, or even violetty – than cognac. The flavour tends to be drier

Above left : Metaxa is the brandy of choice for many holidaymakers. Above right: This top-quality pisco hails from Peru.

because, unlike cognac, armagnac isn't adjusted with sugar, and the absence of caramel as a colouring matter leaves it paler.

The labelling system of armagnac (VS, VSOP, XO) is the same as that of cognac, except that the very youngest armagnacs may be released after two years in cask rather than three. Vintage-dated armagnac – the unblended produce of a single year's harvest – has always been a local peculiarity (although vintage labelling has recently been relegalized in Cognac). If the label on, say, a 1959

armagnac looks suspiciously new, remember that it is because it has probably only recently been bottled. The ageing can only take place in wood, not glass. Prices for even the top armagnacs are considerably gentler than for cognac.

Other European brandies

Spain Brandy production is concentrated in the southern, sherry-producing region of Jerez. Indeed, most Spanish brandy is distilled by the sherry houses. The grapes generally come from the huge central plain of La Mancha, but the wines are distilled and aged in Jerez. Look for "Brandy de Jerez" on the label, as it is a dependable indicator of quality.

Top brands of Spanish brandy include Lepanto, made by Gonzalez Byass, Sanchez Romate's Cardinal Mendoza and Osborne's Conde d'Osborne, which comes in a bottle designed by Salvador Dali. The brand leader is Domecq's commendable Fundador. In Catalonia, the Torres winery makes its own excellent brandies.

Germany The best German offering seen on export markets is Uralt, an aged product made by Asbach in the Rheingau. It receives a maturation period of around 18 months.

Others Italy's brandies are fairly basic commercial spirits. Portugal makes a handful of good brandies, but its industry is heavily geared to supplying grape spirit for the port shippers. Cyprus makes some rough-and-ready brandies too.

Metaxa

Among Greek brandies, the abidingly popular Metaxa deserves a special mention, despite the brouhaha with which it is treated in Greece itself, and a distinctly specious system of age-labelling. There are three grades of Metaxa, ascending in quality from three stars to seven. It is relatively pale in colour and much sweeter on the palate than cognac, with a highly moreish toffee flavour making it taste deceptively light.

American brandies

USA Brandy has been made in the United States since the days of the pioneers, mostly in California. Not all are made in the image of cognac; some are discernibly more Spanish in style. They are matured in American oak, which gives a more pronounced aroma to the spirit, accentuated by the charred inner surfaces of the barrels, and a great richness and complexity on the palate. Star names

Right: A refreshing Pisco Sour is the best way to drink pisco, whether your bottle hails from Chile or Peru.

include Germain-Robin and RMS (the latter owned by Rémy Martin).

Latin America There is a long tradition of fiery spirits all over Central and South America, in which grape brandy plays its part. Mexico is the most important producer. Its flagship is a big-selling global brand called Presidente, made in the light, simple style of basic Spanish brandy.

The peculiarly South American offering, however, is pisco. There is still much dispute over whether it originated in Peru or Chile, the two main centres of production. I shall forbear to come down on either side, except to say that the Pisco valley and its eponymous seaport are in Peru, although the Chileans simply insist that the port was one of the principal export destinations for their spirit, and that consequently the name just stuck.

Despite receiving some cask-ageing, pisco is always colourless because the barrels it matures in are so ancient that they can't tint the spirit. In Chile, the longer the maturation, the lower the dilution

before bottling, so the finest grades (Gran Pisco is the best) are the strongest. Owing to widespread use of the Muscat grape, nearly all types and nationalities of pisco are marked by unabashed fruitiness.

Although it is technically a brandy, pisco should be treated more like the other white spirits – fine vodka and silver tequila. That is to say, it should be mixed, classically as a Pisco Sour, but also with any kind of fruit juice, and served over ice. I have tried it neat at room temperature, but it wasn't a particularly successful experiment.

Cocktail equipment

To be a successful bartender, you will need a few essential pieces of equipment. The most vital and flamboyant is the cocktail shaker.

Cocktail shaker: The shaker is used for drinks that need good mixing but don't have to be crystal-clear. The Boston shaker is made of two cup-type containers that fit over each other, one normally made of glass, the other of metal. This type is often preferred by professional bartenders. For beginners, the classic three-piece shaker is easier to handle, with its base to hold the ice and liquids, a top fitted with a built-in strainer, and a tight-fitting cap. Make sure you hold on to that cap while you are shaking. As a rough rule, the drink is ready when the shaker has become almost too painfully cold to hold, which is generally not more than around 15–20 seconds.

Measure or "jigger": Cocktail shakers usually come with a standard measure – known in American parlance as a "jigger" – for apportioning out the ingredients.

This is usually a single-piece double cup, with one side a whole measure and the other a half.

Measuring jug and spoons: If you don't have a jigger, you can use a jug and/or a set of spoons. The measurements can be in single (25ml/1fl oz) or double (50ml/2fl oz) bar measures.

Blender or liquidizer: Goblet blenders are the best shape for mixing cocktails that need to be aerated, as well as for creating frothy cocktails or ones made with finely crushed ice. Attempting to break up whole ice cubes in the blender may very well blunt the blades. Opt for an ice bag or dish towel, a rolling pin and plenty of brute force, or better still, use an ice crusher.

Ice crusher: This comes in two parts. You fill the top with whole ice cubes, put the lid on and, while pressing down on the top, turn the gramophone-type handle on the side. Take the top half off to retrieve the crystals of ice "snow" from the lower part. Crushed ice is

used to fill the glasses for drinks that are to be served frappé. It naturally melts very quickly, though, compared to cubes.

Wooden hammer: Use a wooden hammer or wooden rolling pin for crushing ice.

Towel or ice bag A clean towel or bag is essential for holding ice cubes when crushing.

Ice bucket: An ice bucket is useful if you are going to be making several cocktails in succession. They are not completely hermetic though, and ice will eventually melt in them, albeit a little more slowly than if left at room temperature.

Mixing pitcher or bar glass: It is useful to have a container in which to mix and stir drinks that are not shaken. The pitcher or bar glass should be large enough to hold two or three drinks. This vessel is intended for drinks that are meant to be clear, not cloudy.

Bar spoon: These long-handled spoons can reach to the bottom of the tallest tumblers and are used in jugs, or for mixing the drink directly in the glass. Some varieties of bar spoon look like a large swizzle-stick, with a long spiral-shaped handle and a disc at one end.

Muddler: A long stick with a bulbous end, the muddler is used for crushing sugar or mint leaves, and so is particularly useful when creating juleps or smashes. A variety of sizes is available.

Strainer: Used for pouring drinks from a shaker or mixing jug into a cocktail glass, the strainer's function is to remove the ice with which the drink has been prepared. The best-known is called a Hawthorn strainer. It is made from stainless steel and looks like a flat spoon with holes and a curl of wire on the underside. It is held over the top of the glass to keep the ice and any other solid ingredients back.

Corkscrew: The fold-up type of corkscrew is known as the Waiter's Friend, and incorporates a can opener and bottle-top flipper as well as the screw itself. It is the most useful version to have to hand.

Sharp knife and squeezer: Citrus fruit is essential in countless cocktails. A good quality, sharp knife is required for halving the fruit, and the squeezer for extracting its juice.

Nutmeg grater: A tiny grater with small holes, for grating nutmeg over frothy and creamy drinks.

Zester and canelle knife: These are used for presenting fruit attractively to garnish glasses. The zester has a row of tiny holes that remove the top layer of skin off a citrus fruit when dragged across it (although the finest gauge on your multi-purpose grater was also designed for just this job).

A canelle knife is for making decorative stripes in the skins of a whole fruit. When sliced, they then have an attractive serrated edge.

Egg whisk: Use a whisk to beat a little frothy texture into egg white

Above: You can amass cocktail equipment over time.

before you add it to the shaker. It helps the texture of the drink.

Cocktail and swizzle-sticks: Cocktail sticks are mainly decorative, used for holding ingredients such as olives that would otherwise sink to the bottom of the glass. And if you intend to eat the olive, it's handier if it's already speared, so that you don't have to commit the appalling faux pas of dipping a finger into the drink to catch it. A swizzle-stick is useful for stirring a drink, and may be substituted by a stick of celery or cucumber.

Glasses

To ensure that glasses are sparkling clean, they should always be washed and dried with a glass cloth. Although some recipes suggest chilled glasses, don't put best crystal in the freezer; leave it at the back of the refrigerator instead. An hour should be enough.

Collins glass or highball
The tallest of the tumblers, narrow with perfectly straight sides, a Collins glass holds about 350ml/

Left: Collins glass

12fl oz, and is usually used for serving long drinks made with fresh juices or finished with a sparkling mixer such as soda. This glass can also stand in as the highball glass, which is traditionally slightly less tall Uses: Morning Glory Fizz, Apple Sour, Fighter and Never on Sunday.

Cocktail glass or Martini glass
This elegant glass is a wide conical bowl on a tall stem: a design that keeps cocktails cool by keeping warm hands away from the drink. It is by far the most widely used glass, so a set is essential. The design belies the fact that the capacity of this glass is relatively small (about three standard measures). Uses: Vanderbilt, Corpse Reviver, Lemon Lady, and almost any short, sharp, strong cocktail, including creamy ones.

Left: Cocktail glass or Martini glass

Above: Balloon glass

Brandy balloon or snifter
The brandy glass is designed to trap the fragrance of the brandy in the bowl of the glass, although these days it is thought that the aromas are better appreciated in something resembling a large liqueur glass, which mutes the prickle of the 40% raw spirit. It nonetheless makes a good cocktail glass for certain short, strong drinks that have been stirred rather than shaken. The wide bowl makes them suitable for drinks with solids floating in them. Uses: B&B and Missile Stopper.

Large cocktail goblet
Available in various sizes and shapes, large cocktail goblets are good for serving larger frothy

Above: Large cocktail goblet and champagne saucer.

cracked ice floating in them. Because of the wider surface are, there is plenty of scope for fruity garnishes too. Uses: Frozen Strawberry Daiquiri, Bombay and Last Goodbye.

Tumbler or rocks glass

Classic, short whisky tumblers are used for shorter drinks, served on the rocks, and generally for drinks that are stirred rather than shaken. They should hold about 250ml/8fl oz. Uses: Brandy Smash, Brandy Fix, East India, Block and Fall, Sidecar and Incredible.

Liqueur glass

Tiny liqueur glasses were traditionally used to serve small measures of unmixed drinks, and hold no more than 80ml/3fl oz. Uses: Savoy Hotel, and Airstrike.

Even clean glasses should be rinsed out and wiped before use, because glasses that have been stored for any length of time can acquire a dusty taste.

drinks, or drinks containing puréed fruit or coconut cream. The wider rim of this type of glass leaves plenty of room for flamboyant and colourful decorations. Uses: Brandy Melba and Olympic.

Champagne saucer

The old-fashioned saucer glass may be frowned on now for champagne, but it is an attractive and elegant design and can be used for a number of cocktails, particularly those that have

Right: Tumbler or rocks glass and liqueur glass

Presentation is important – elegant cocktail glasses look even better when served with clean, white linen cloths.

Tricks of the trade

It is worth mastering the techniques for the preparation of good-looking drinks. The following pages give you precise directions for some of the essential procedures, such as crushing ice and shaking cocktails.

Crushing ice

It isn't a good idea to break ice up in a blender or food processor as you may find it damages the blades. Instead do the following:

1 Lay out a clean glass cloth or dish towel, on a work surface, and cover half of it with ice cubes. (If you wish, you can also use a cloth ice bag.)

2 Fold the cloth over and, using a rolling pin or mallet, smash down on the ice firmly several times, until you achieve the required fineness.

3 Spoon the ice into glasses or a pitcher. Fine ice snow must be used immediately because it melts, but cracked or roughly crushed ice can be stored in the freezer in plastic bags.

Shaking cocktails

Cocktails that contain sugar syrups or creams require more than just a stir; they are combined and chilled with a brief shake. Remember that it is possible to shake only one or two servings at any one time, so you may have to work quickly in batches. It is important to always use fresh ice each time.

1 Add four or five ice cubes to the shaker and pour in all the ingredients.

2 Put the lid on the shaker. Hold the shaker firmly in one hand, keeping the lid in place with the other hand.

3 Shake vigorously for about 15 seconds to blend simple concoctions, and for 20–30 seconds for drinks with sugar syrups or cream. The shaker should feel extremely cold.

4 Remove the small cap and pour into the prepared glass, using a strainer if the shaker is not already fitted with one.

Brandy Smash

The excitingly named Smash is essentially a miniaturized julep (or Mint Julep). It may be made with any spirit, but is particularly successful with brandy.

5ml/1 tsp caster (superfine) sugar
4 mint leaves
2 measures/3 tbsp cognac
1 measure/1½ tbsp soda water

Dissolve the sugar in a little water in a tumbler. Add the mint leaves and press them into the sugar solution to express some of the juices. Put in a couple of ice cubes, and then add the brandy and stir vigorously. Add the soda. Squeeze a piece of lemon over the top of the drink, and decorate with a half-slice of orange.

Bartending know-how
Mint lends a smack of herbal goodness to a range of cocktails. Be sure to use only the freshest leaves.

Frosting glasses
The appearance and taste of a cocktail are enhanced if the rim of your glass is frosted. After frosting, place the glass in the refrigerator to chill until needed.

1 Hold the glass upside down, so the juice does not run down the glass. Rub the rim with the cut surface of a lemon, lime, orange or even a slice of fresh pineapple.

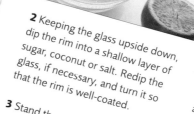

2 Keeping the glass upside down, dip the rim into a shallow layer of sugar, coconut or salt. Redip the glass, if necessary, and turn it so that the rim is well-coated.

3 Stand the glass upright and let it sit until the sugar, coconut or salt has dried on the rim, then chill.

Making twists
As an alternative to slices of the fruit, drinks can be garnished with a twist of orange, lemon or lime rind. Twists should be made before the drink itself is prepared, so that you don't keep a cold cocktail waiting. Here's how:

1 Choose a citrus fruit with an unblemished skin and a regular shape.

2 Using a canelle knife or potato peeler, start at the tip of the fruit and start peeling round, as though you were peeling an apple.

3 Work slowly and carefully down the fruit, being sure to keep the pared-away rind in one continuous strip.

4 Trim it, if necessary, to a length that suits the glass.

5 A long twist in a cocktail glass makes the drink look sophisticated and elegant, and is

the cocktails

Vanderbilt

This cocktail was created in 1912 in honour of Cornelius Vanderbilt, member of one of America's great plutocratic families. The flavour is certainly rich enough to do justice to the name.

1½ measures/2 tbsp cognac
½ measure/2 tsp cherry brandy
2 dashes Angostura bitters
¼ measure/1 tsp sugar syrup

Shake all the ingredients well with ice, and strain into a cocktail glass. Garnish with a twist of lemon, and a couple of cocktail cherries on a cocktail stick.

Brandy Blazer

A warming after-dinner tipple,
this is ideally served with fresh
vanilla ice cream or caramelized
oranges.

½ orange
1 lemon
2 measures/3 tbsp cognac
1 sugar cube
½ measure/2 tsp Kahlúa

Pare the rind from the orange and
lemon, removing and discarding as
much of the white pith as possible.
Put the cognac, sugar cube, lemon
and orange rind in a small pan. Heat
gently, then remove from the heat,
light a match and pass the flame
close to the surface of the liquid.
The alcohol will burn with a low,
blue flame for about a minute. Blow
out the flame. Add the Kahlúa to
the pan, and strain into a heat-
resistant glass. Garnish with a
cocktail stick threaded with orange
rind, and serve warm.

Brandy Alexander

One of the greatest cocktails of them all, Alexander can be served at the end of a grand dinner with coffee as a creamy digestif, or as the first drink of the evening at a cocktail party, since the cream in it helps to line the stomach. It was possibly originally made with gin rather than brandy, and the cream was sweetened, but the formula below is undoubtedly the best of all possible worlds.

1 measure/1½ tbsp cognac
1 measure/1½ tbsp brown crème de cacao
1 measure/1½ tbsp double (heavy) cream

Shake the ingredients thoroughly with ice, and strain into a cocktail glass. Scatter ground nutmeg, or grate a little whole nutmeg, on top. Alternatively, sprinkle with grated dark chocolate.

Brandy Cocktail

Over time, this drink became modified to include Cointreau instead of curaçao, a little sugar syrup and a dash of Angostura. However, the earliest versions of it are nothing more than cognac with a soupçon of bitterness.

1½ measures/2 tbsp cognac
2 dashes orange curaçao

Stir the ingredients gently with ice in a bar glass, and then strain into a brandy balloon. Do not garnish.

B&B

The traditional mix of this world-famous cocktail is half-and-half Bénédictine and good brandy (cognac for preference), stirred not shaken, and not usually iced. In fact, for true authenticity, you don't even need a stirrer. The two drinks are simply poured into a balloon glass, the brandy first, and the drink swirled in the hand before being passed to its recipient. No garnish is needed. Just relax and enjoy.

Bartending know-how
Bénédictine is a cognac-based herbal liqueur originally formulated by Dom Bernardo, a Benedictine monk. It is a bright golden potion of honeyed, spicy sweetness, containing a herbalist's pantheon of medicinal plants and spices which are left to infuse in a base of cognac. The resulting potion is then re-distilled to concentrate the flavour.

Brandy Fix

A 'fix' is a mixture of spirit with lemon juice, sweetening, and in this case another alcohol flavour, with the shell of the lemon and a pile of ice left in the drink for good measure.

5ml/1 tsp sugar
juice and rind of half a lemon
1½ measures/2 tbsp cognac
¾ measure/1 tbsp cherry brandy

Dissolve the sugar in a little water in the bottom of a small tumbler, and then fill it with crushed ice. Add the lemon juice and alcohol and stir the drink well. Drop in the squeezed lemon rind.

Corpse Reviver 1

This was the 1920s idea of a morning-after remedy, and is probably the first recipe that can lay claim to this name. It looks much more like a night-before drink to me – and a good one at that.

1½ measures/2 tbsp cognac
¾ measure/1 tbsp calvados
¾ measure/1 tbsp sweet red
*   vermouth*

Shake all the ingredients well with ice, and strain into a cocktail glass. Again, no garnish is required.

Corpse Reviver 2

Not the most delicately named
cocktail, this is a 1970s recipe
intended of course as another
morning-after remedy. I'm not
sure I'd make quite that claim for
it myself, but in its bitterly minty
way, it tastes convincingly
medicinal, which is what matters
at such times.

1 measure/1½ tbsp cognac
1 measure/1½ tbsp Fernet Branca
1 measure/1½ tbsp white crème de
    menthe

Shake all the ingredients well with
ice, and strain into a cocktail glass.
Do not garnish. If you really are
taking it at 10 o'clock in the
morning, you're not likely to care
about twists of this and slices of
that anyway.

Morning Glory Fizz

A good early-morning drink, this should be consumed as soon as it is made, before it loses its bubbles.

³/₄ measure/1 tbsp cognac
¼ measure/1 tsp orange curaçao
¼ measure/1 tsp lemon juice
dash anisette
2 dashes Angostura bitters
4 measures/6 tbsp soda water

Shake all but the last ingredient well with ice, and strain into a chilled highball glass. Finish with the soda water. Garnish the drink with a twist of lemon rind.

Frozen Strawberry Daiquiri

This is a spinoff version of the
rum original. When the fresh
fruit isn't in season, use drained,
canned strawberries instead, but
wash off the sugar syrup.

4 strawberries
½ measure/2 tsp lime juice
1 measure/1½ tbsp cognac
1 measure/1½ tbsp light rum
dash grenadine

Put the strawberries, lime juice and
brandy in a liquidizer and process
to a purée. Add the light rum,
grenadine and half a glass of finely
crushed ice and process once more
to a smooth slush. Pour the
resulting mixture into a well-chilled
cocktail glass. Garnish with a
strawberry and a small sprig of
fresh mint, if you like.

Connoisseur's Treat

Certainly a treat for somebody, this is a very strong, all-alcohol mix, not to be taken lightly. The flavour is a heady combination of herbs, vanilla and orange.

1½ measures/2 tbsp cognac
½ measure/2 tsp Grand Marnier
½ measure/2 tsp Galliano

Stir the ingredients in a pitcher with ice until thoroughly chilled, and strain into a rocks glass. Garnish with a slice of orange.

Bartending know-how
Galliano was invented in 1896 by Arturo Vaccari. The formula is a closely guarded secret but it is said to be based on over 30 herbs, roots, berries and flowers from the alpine slopes to the north of Italy. It is naturally very sweet with a pronounced scent of vanilla and anise overtones.

Bombay

A very strong and challenging mixture, this is the kind of drink that comes in handy in situations where Dutch courage is called for. Or should that be Indian courage?

1½ measures/2 tbsp cognac
¾ measures/1 tbsp dry vermouth
¾ measure/1 tbsp sweet red
  vermouth
¼ measure/1 tsp Cointreau
¼ measure/1 tsp absinthe

Shake all the ingredients well with ice, and strain into a cocktail glass or champagne saucer filled with crushed ice. Do not garnish.

Apple Sour

For those who don't fancy swallowing raw egg, this drink can be made without the egg white. Applejack or apple schnapps also work well in place of the calvados.

1 measure/1½ tbsp cognac
1 measure/1½ tbsp calvados
³/4 measure/1 tbsp lemon juice
5ml/1 tsp sugar
dash Angostura bitters
1 egg white

Shake all the ingredients well with ice, and strain into a tall glass half-filled with cracked ice. Garnish the drink with slices of red and green apple dipped in lemon juice.

Bartending know-how
When using egg white in any cocktail, make sure the egg is very fresh.

Pisco Sour

The origin of pisco, the colourless brandy of South America, is energetically disputed between Peru and Chile. This is the classic way of taking it locally. As with the Apple Sour, you can make the drink with or without the egg white.

juice of half a lime
5ml/1 tsp caster (superfine) sugar
2 measures/3 tbsp pisco

Half-fill a small tumbler with smashed ice. Squeeze the lime juice directly into the glass and drop in the wrung-out shell. Add the sugar and stir well to dissolve it. Now add the pisco, and give the drink a stir. A dash of Angostura bitters can be added too, if desired. Garnish with a slice of lime.

East India

This short and elegant drink can be served as an aperitif, as it has a pleasantly bitter note to it.

³/₄ measure/1 tbsp cognac
¹/₄ measure/1 tsp white curaçao
2 dashes pineapple juice
2 dashes Angostura bitters

Stir all the ingredients well with ice in a pitcher until chilled, and strain into a small tumbler or rocks glass, half-filled with broken ice. Garnish with a twist of lime.

Cranberry Kiss

In this delicious, full-flavoured cocktail, the tang of cranberry and pink grapefruit juices is balanced by the toffeeish sweetness of marsala.

redcurrants, to garnish
1 egg white, lightly beaten, and
    15ml/1 tbsp caster (superfine)
    sugar, to garnish
1 measure/1½ tbsp cognac
2 measures/3 tbsp cranberry juice
2 measures/3 tbsp pink grapefruit
    juice
2 measures/3 tbsp marsala dolce

For the garnish, lightly brush the redcurrants with the egg white. Shake sugar over them to cover with a frosting. Set aside to dry. Shake the brandy and cranberry and grapefruit juices with ice and strain into a well-chilled cocktail glass. Tilt the glass slightly before slowly pouring in the marsala down the side. Garnish with the frosted redcurrants.

Never on Sunday

This recipe uses Metaxa, the softly caramelly Greek brandy, together with its compatriot, aniseedy ouzo, for a thoroughly delightful Mediterranean experience.

1 measure/1½ tbsp Metaxa
½ measure/2 tsp ouzo
dash lemon juice
dash Angostura bitters
2 measures/3 tbsp dry sparkling
    wine
2 measures/3 tbsp sparkling ginger
    ale

Stir the first four ingredients in a pitcher with ice, strain into a tall glass and top up with the sparkling wine and ginger ale. Garnish with a slice of lemon.

Port Side

The purply-red colour of this sophisticated short drink looks very fetching sinking through a snowdrift of crushed ice.

1½ measures/2 tbsp cognac
½ measure/2 tsp ruby port
½ measure/2 tsp crème de mûre

Stir all the ingredients with ice in a pitcher, and strain into a rocks glass half-filled with crushed ice. Garnish with a blackberry, if you happen to have one to hand.

Bartending know-how
Crème de mûre is a richly sweet dark purple liqueur made from blackberries, red wine, sugar and brandy.

Lemon Lady

This is a delightful concoction that will have guests coming back for more. It could be served between courses as a more invigorating alternative to a straight sorbet.

1 measure/1½ tbsp cognac
½ measure/2 tsp Cointreau
3 measures/4½ tbsp light, partially melted lemon sorbet

Shake the ingredients well with ice to combine the sorbet, and strain into a chilled cocktail glass. Garnish with a slice of lemon.

Missile Stopper

On a military hardware theme, this fruity little number should stop anyone in their tracks.

1 measure/1½ tbsp cognac
½ measure/2 tsp crème de fraise
1 measure/1½ tbsp grapefruit juice
1 measure/1½ tbsp pineapple juice
¼ measure/1 tsp grenadine

Shake all the ingredients well with ice, and strain into a chilled balloon glass. Garnish with a sliver of pineapple and strawberry slices.

Bartending know-how
Grenadine is a (usually) non-alcoholic syrup made principally from the juice of the pomegranate. It is thick, ruby-coloured and intensely sweet. Just a small amount is needed to give your cocktail a rich crimson colour.

Incredible

Chartreuse doesn't often mix well with other spirits, but this is definitely worth a go, incredible as it may seem.

1 measure/1½ tbsp cognac
½ measure/2 tsp green Chartreuse
½ measure/2 tsp cherry brandy

Stir all the ingredients gently with ice in a pitcher until well-chilled, and then strain into a rocks glass. Garnish with a cocktail cherry.

Bartending know-how
Unlike Bénédictine, Chartreuse really is still made by monks, who make it at Voiron, near Grenoble. It is sold as green (55%) and yellow (40%). Green Chartreuse is a leafy colour, has a pungent herbal scent and is less viscous than the yellow variety. By varying processes of distillation, infusion and maceration, over 130 herbs and plants are used to flavour a base of grape brandy. It is then aged in casks for up to five years.

Pompeii

Here is a different spin on the Alexander formula (see page 21), but with the chocolate component given a sweeter, nutty edge.

1 measure/1½ tbsp cognac
¾ measure/1 tbsp white crème de cacao
½ measure/2 tsp amaretto
1 measure/1½ tbsp double (heavy) cream

Shake all the ingredients well with ice, and strain into a cocktail glass. Sprinkle the drink's surface with flaked almonds.

Champarelle

Dating from the late 19th century, this is one of the oldest recipes for the layered drink known as a pousse-café. It helps if the ingredients and the glass itself are pre-chilled, as they are not mixed in any way, and you can't put ice in the drink.

½ measure/2 tsp orange curaçao
½ measure/2 tsp yellow Chartreuse
½ measure/2 tsp anisette
½ measure/2 tsp cognac

Carefully pour each of the ingredients in this order over the back of a large spoon into a liqueur glass or sherry schooner, ensuring that they remain in separate layers. Use a clean spoon

Blackjack

Perhaps invented to steady nerves at the gaming table, this mix is more likely to impair concentration. It is a stimulating one nonetheless.

1 measure/1½ tbsp cognac
½ measure/2 tsp kirsch
½ measure/2 tsp Kahlúa
2 measures/3 tbsp cold black coffee

Shake all the ingredients well with ice, and pour without straining into a rocks glass. Do not garnish.

Bartending know-how
Kirsch made in Germany tends to be drier and higher in alcohol than the versions made in the Alsace region of France.

Fighter

This combative mixture is rendered seemingly tamer by the sparkling top-up. Do not be deceived.

1 measure/1½ tbsp cognac
½ measure/2 tsp vodka
½ measure/2 tsp Mandarine
  Napoléon
4 measures/6 tbsp sparkling bitter
  lemon

Add the first three ingredients to a highball glass half-filled with cracked ice. Stir vigorously. Top up with the bitter lemon. Garnish with a slice of mandarin orange, clementine, satsuma or similar.

Bayou

The peachiness of this cocktail evokes the southern United States, as does its name. It is rich and fruity, with a refreshing sour finish.

1½ measures/2 tbsp cognac
½ measure/2 tsp peach brandy
1 measure/1½ tbsp peach juice
⅓ measure/1½ tsp lime juice

Shake all the ingredients well with ice, and strain into a rocks glass. Garnish with slices of ultra-ripe peach.

Bartending know-how
Peach brandy is one of the less well-known fruit liqueurs. The pressed juice and stones of peach are mixed with a neutral grape spirit, sweetened with sugar syrup, and macerated until the take-up of the flavour is complete.

Apricot Bellini

This is a version of the famous aperitif served at Harry's Bar in Venice. Instead of sparkling wine and peach juice, apricot nectar and apricot brandy make this a stronger variation. It serves 6-8.

3 ripe apricots
½ measure/2 tsp lemon juice
½ measure/2 tsp sugar syrup
1 measure/1½ tbsp cognac
1 measure/1½ tbsp apricot brandy
1 bottle brut champagne or dry
    sparkling wine, chilled

Plunge the apricots into boiling water for 2 minutes to loosen the skins, then peel and pit them. Discard the pits and skin. Process the apricot flesh with the lemon juice until you have a smooth purée. Sweeten to taste with sugar syrup, then strain. Add the brandy to the apricot liqueur and stir together. Divide the apricot nectar among chilled champagne flutes. Finish the drinks with chilled champagne or sparkling wine.

Captain Kidd

Brandy and dark rum make a heady, but very successful mix in a powerful cocktail, and this one is further enhanced by the addition of strong chocolate flavour. There are no non-alcoholic ingredients, you'll notice, so watch out.

1½ measures/2 tbsp cognac
1 measure/1½ tbsp dark rum
1 measure/1½ tbsp brown crème
    de cacao

Shake well with ice, and strain into a chilled champagne saucer. Garnish with a physalis or a half-slice of orange.

Savoy Hotel

One of the spiritual homes of the cocktail is the American Bar at London's Savoy Hotel, where this delightful cocktail (like many another) was created. It's a pousse-café or layered drink that requires a steady hand.

1 measure/1½ tbsp brown crème de cacao
1 measure/1½ tbsp Bénédictine
1 measure/1½ tbsp cognac

Carefully pour each of the ingredients, in this order, over the back of a spoon into a liqueur glass or sherry schooner to create a multi-layered drink. Serve immediately, while the effect is intact.

Dizzy Dame

Well, she will be after drinking two or three of these. Another of those creamy cocktails full of rich, indulgent flavours (and calories).

1 measure/1½ tbsp cognac
¾ measure/1 tbsp Tia Maria
½ measure/2 tsp cherry brandy
¾ measure/1 tbsp double (heavy) cream

Shake all the ingredients well with ice, and strain into a cocktail glass. Garnish with a cocktail cherry.

Bartending know-how
Tia Maria is a suave, deep brown coffee-flavoured drink, based on a recipe around three centuries old. It is made using good, dark Jamaican rum of at least five years old and flavoured with the beans of the highly prized coffee variety, Blue Mountain. The palate is further deepened by the addition of aromatic spices including vanilla.

Harvard

This mixture was invented at the distinguished Ivy League university in the 1920s. It originally had equal quantities of brandy and vermouth and no lemon juice, but this is a less sweet and altogether more balanced mixture.

1½ measures/2 tbsp cognac
½ measure/2 tsp sweet red
  vermouth
¼ measure/1 tsp lemon juice
¼ measure/1 tsp grenadine
2 dashes Angostura bitters

Shake all the ingredients well with ice, and strain into a cocktail glass. Garnish with a twist of lemon.

Lake Como

The geographical reference recalls the origins of the excellent Italian liqueur used in this recipe.

1½ measures/2 tbsp cognac
¾ measure/1 tbsp Tuaca

Mix the ingredients well with ice in a large glass, and strain into a small rocks glass. Squeeze a twist of lemon rind over the drink and then drop it into the glass. This is one for drinking quickly and confidently.

Bartending know-how
Tuaca is an Italian liqueur made up of orange essence and vanilla on a base of Italian brandy. It is not excessively sweet and makes an excellent single shot taken neat as well as being a good blending partner at the cocktail bar.

Brandy Melba

As might be expected, this is a very fruity cocktail that could almost pass as a sort of dessert. It uses the combination of peach and raspberry in the classic Peach Melba dessert.

1½ measures/2 tbsp cognac
½ measure/2 tsp peach schnapps
¼ measure/1 tsp crème de framboise
½ measure/2 tsp lemon juice
¼ measure/1 tsp orange bitters (or curaçao)

Shake well with ice, and strain into a chilled cocktail glass. Garnish with a slice of ripe peach and a raspberry.

Kiss the Boys Goodbye

As the name suggests, this is a cocktail with which American troops going off to serve in the Second World War were toasted. It seemed to do the trick.

1 measure/1½ tbsp cognac
1 measure/1½ tbsp sloe gin
¼ measure/1 tsp lemon juice
½ egg white

Shake all the ingredients well with ice, and strain into a rocks glass half-filled with cracked ice. Garnish with a wedge of lemon.

Sidecar

Cointreau can successfully be mixed with virtually any spirit (except perhaps whisky) and a quantity of lemon juice, and shaken with ice. Start with gin and you have a White Lady, vodka for a Balalaika and even tequila for a lemon Margarita. The brandy version is a Paris classic called Sidecar, after the preferred means of travel of a French army officer.

1½ measures/2 tbsp cognac
¾ measure/1 tbsp Cointreau
¾ measure/1 tbsp lemon juice

Shake well with ice and strain into a rocks glass with a little cracked ice. Garnish with a half-slice of lemon.

Stinger

The adaptable Stinger is simply a two-thirds-one-third mixture of any spirit with white crème de menthe, shaken with ice and served over smashed ice in a cocktail glass. The prototype version, dating from around the time of the First World War, is with cognac, as in the following recipe.

2 measures/3 tbsp cognac
1 measure/1½ tbsp white crème de menthe

Shake both the ingredients well with ice, and strain into a cocktail glass. You could garnish it with a tuft of mint, although it is fine without.

Bartending know-how
The principal flavouring element in crème de menthe – green or white – is peppermint. Its flavour is more subtly aromatic and refreshing than that of spearmint.

Hazelnut Whirl

This one sounds and, for that matter, tastes as though it ought to be lurking somewhere in the bottom layer of a box of fine chocolates.

1 measure/1½ tbsp cognac
1 measure/1½ tbsp crème de noisette
1 measure/1½ tbsp double (heavy) cream

Shake all the ingredients well with ice, and strain into a cocktail glass. Garnish with a sprinkling of grated dark chocolate and a walnut half.

Block and Fall

Cocktails that include pastis tend to be the most dramatic in the repertoire. Many of these contain no non-alcoholic ingredients. That is because a relatively small amount of pastis will have plenty to say for itself in even the most ferocious of mixes, concoctions that would drown the presence of many of the more delicate liqueurs.

1 measure/1½ tbsp cognac
1 measure/1½ tbsp Cointreau
½ measure/2 tsp Pernod
½ measure/2 tsp calvados

Stir all the ingredients together with ice in a pitcher, and then strain into a tumbler half-filled with cracked ice. Add a slice of lemon.

Sunburn

A dark and brooding combination of brandy and coffee liqueur is brightened up with fresh citrus juices. The effect is an unusual one, but you will find that you have grown to love it by the time you finish the drink.

1 measure/1½ tbsp cognac
1 measure/1½ tbsp Tia Maria
½ measure/2 tsp orange juice
½ measure/2 tsp lemon juice

Shake all the ingredients well with ice, and strain into a cocktail glass. Garnish with half-slices of orange and lemon.

Torpedo

I have come across various different mixtures going under this title. This seems to me to be the one most worthy of the name. It's very dry, spirity and strong, and its name reflects something of the force with which it will go through you.

1½ measures/2 tbsp cognac
¾ measure/1 tbsp calvados
dash gin

Shake all the ingredients well with ice, and strain into a pre-chilled cocktail glass. Garnish with a twist of lemon.

Via Veneto

Named after the street in Rome that was once a scene of bohemian glamour, this cocktail contains the Italian elderberry-flavoured liqueur Sambuca Romana.

1½ measures/2 tbsp cognac
½ measure/2 tsp Sambuca
½ measure/2 tsp lemon juice
¼ measure/1 tsp sugar syrup
½ egg white

Shake all the ingredients well with ice, and strain into a chilled rocks glass. Garnish with a slice of lemon.

Sundowner

This recipe uses the bitter, orange-flavoured South African liqueur, Van der Hum, in a variation on the formula for Sunburn (see page 53). Instead of using cognac, though, you could substitute a good South African brandy if you come across it. Many of them are surprisingly fine in quality.

1½ measures/2 tbsp cognac
1 measure/1½ tbsp Van der Hum
½ measure/2 tsp orange juice
½ measure/2 tsp lemon juice

Shake all the ingredients well with ice, and strain into a cocktail glass. Garnish with a physalis fruit.

Olympic

Created for the 1924 Olympic
Games in Paris, this is a gold
medal-winning recipe.

1 measure/1½ tbsp cognac
1 measure/1½ tbsp orange curaçao
1 measure/1½ tbsp orange juice

Shake all the ingredients well with
ice, and strain into a cocktail glass.
Garnish with a twist of orange rind.

Bartending know-how
Citrus twists are relatively easy
to make once you've had a bit
of practice. Cut thin strips of
orange or lemon rind and then
curl them tightly around a thin
wooden stick. Slide the stick
out and you have your twist.

Last Goodbye

The flavours of cherry brandy and Cointreau are seen as being particularly compatible with cognac, and this is another appealing mixture.

1 measure/1½ tbsp cognac
¾ measure/1 tbsp cherry brandy
¼ measure/1 tsp Cointreau
½ measure/2 tsp lime juice
¼ measure/1 tsp grenadine

Shake all the ingredients well with ice, and strain into a balloon glass. You could garnish with a lime slice and a cherry.

Bartending know-how
One of the most popular branded liqueurs of all, Cointreau is, properly speaking, a variety of curaçao. This means it is a brandy-based spirit that has been flavoured with the rind of bitter oranges. Despite its 40% strength, Cointreau tastes deliciously innocuous.

Arago

This delightful creamy creation is quite as irresistible as the Pompeii (see page 37).

1½ measures/2 tbsp cognac
1 measure/1½ tbsp crème de
  banane
1 measure/1½ tbsp double (heavy)
  cream

Shake all the ingredients well with ice, and strain into a cocktail glass. Sprinkle the surface of the drink with grated dark chocolate.

Airstrike

This is a burning drink, similar to the Italian flaming Sambuca tradition.

2 measures/3 tbsp Galliano
1 measure/1½ tbsp cognac
1 star anise

Heat the Galliano and brandy in a small pan until just warm. Pour into a heat resistant liqueur glass and add the star anise. Using a long match, pass the flame over the surface of the drink to ignite it, being careful not to burn yourself. Let it burn for a couple of minutes, until the star anise has begun to sizzle a little and released its aroma into the drink. Leave to cool slightly before drinking.

Memphis Belle

One of the earliest cocktail recipes to use Southern Comfort, this may look an unlikely idea, in that it blends a whiskey-based liqueur with brandy, but in its dry, sharply sour way, it works.

1½ measures/2 tbsp cognac
¾ measure/1 tbsp Southern
  Comfort
½ measure/2 tsp lemon juice
¼ measure/1 tsp orange bitters (or
  curaçao)

Shake all the ingredients well with ice, and strain into a pre-chilled cocktail glass. Garnish with a twist of lemon.

Bordeaux Cocktail

A good way of disguising any harshness in a young red wine,
this recipe is classically made with a young claret from Bordeaux.
Wine-tasters claim to find the taste of blackcurrant in the Cabernet
Sauvignon grape that much claret contains, but you can make sure of
that by adding the blackcurrant liqueur, cassis.

2 measures/3 tbsp red Bordeaux
1 measure/1½ tbsp cognac
¾ measure/1 tbsp crème de cassis

Stir all the ingredients well with ice
in a pitcher, and strain into a large
wine glass. Do not garnish.

Coffee Cognac Cooler

This drink is unabashedly decadent, and not for those counting
calories. The recipe serves two, so you can both feel guilty together.

250ml/8fl oz cold strong dark-roast
* coffee*
80ml/3fl oz cognac
50ml/2fl oz coffee liqueur
50ml/2fl oz double (heavy) cream
10ml/2 tsp sugar
2 scoops coffee ice cream

Shake or blend all the ingredients
except the ice cream together with
plenty of crushed ice. Pour into
cocktail glasses and gently add a
scoop of ice cream to each. Garnish
with chocolate shavings.

Coffee and Chocolate Flip

Use only the freshest egg in this recipe, as it isn't cooked. The result is a smoothly frothy, intensely rich drink. The chocolate element is confined to the garnish.

1 egg
5ml/1 tsp sugar
1 measure/1½ tbsp cognac
1 measure/1½ tbsp Kahlúa
5ml/1 tsp dark-roast instant coffee granules
3 measures/4½ tbsp double (heavy) cream
cocoa powder, to garnish

Separate the egg and lightly beat the white until frothy. In a separate bowl, beat the egg yolk with the sugar. In a small pan, combine the brandy, Kahlúa, coffee and cream and warm over a very low heat. Allow the mixture to cool, then whisk it into the egg yolk. Add the egg white to the egg and cream, and pour the mixture briefly back and forth between two glasses until it is smooth. Pour into a tall glass over coarsely crushed ice and sprinkle the top with cocoa powder.

Index

This edition is published by Lorenz Books, an imprint of Anness Publishing Ltd
info @anness.com
www.annesspublishing.com

© Anness Publishing 2018

A CIP catalogue record for this book is available from the British Library.

Publisher: Joanna Lorenz
Editorial Director: Helen Sudell
Photographers: Frank Adam, Steve Baxter, Janine Hosegood, Jon Whitaker
Designer: Nigel Partridge
Production Controller: Ben Worley

PUBLISHER'S NOTE
Although the advice and information in this book are believed to be accurate and true at the time of going to press, neither the authors nor the publisher can accept any legal responsibility of liability for any errors or omissions that may have been made nor for any inaccuracies nor for any loss, harm or injury that comes about from following instructions or advice in this book.

DRINK AWARENESS
Always drink legally and responsibly. Do not drink and drive, and avoid alcohol whilst pregnant or trying to conceive.